THEN & NOW

PEABODY

Opposite: When Giles Corey was tried as a wizard in 1692, he stood mute pleading neither guilty nor innocent. This action, while guaranteeing a guilty verdict, protected his land and assets from seizure by the court. Before his death, he deeded part of his land currently around Oak Grove Cemetery to his daughter and son-in-law John Moulton. The house, built around 1650, was left unattended and finally destroyed by fire in 1966. This striking photograph is from the dawn of the last century.

PEABODY

William R. Power

To the hardworking and dedicated members of Peabody's historical community, both past and present, who have made it their mission to preserve the historic character of our city. Especially Jack Wells, Theodore Moody Osborne, and J. W. Hanson, all of whom have written books on Peabody history and have made the road a lot easier for those of us who follow.

ISBN 978-0-7385-5546-1

Library of Congress control number: 2007932889

Published by Arcadia Publishing
Charleston SC, Chicago IL, Portsmouth NH, San Francisco CA

Printed in the United States of America

For all general information contact Arcadia Publishing at:
Telephone 843-853-2070
Fax 843-853-0044
E-mail sales@arcadiapublishing.com
For customer service and orders:
Toll-Free 1-888-313-2665

Visit us on the Internet at www.arcadiapublishing.com

On the front cover: Please see page 41. (Vintage photograph, courtesy Peabody Historical Society and Museum; contemporary photograph, author's collection.)

On the back cover: Please see page 78. (Courtesy Peabody Historical Society and Museum.)

Contents

Acknowledgments

I would like to acknowledge the real stars of this story: those individuals who traveled through their neighborhoods at the dawn of the 20th century trying out the latest technology, the Kodak camera. While photography had been around for many years, until this time there was no real camera for the masses. Once available, people joyfully embraced the ability to rather easily document their lives and the lives of those around them on film. Their pictorial legacy serves as the basis of the concept of the Then & Now series.

Additionally, I recognize the kind assistance of the Peabody Historical Society and Museum's curator Heather Leavell; society historian Barbara Doucette, who is always cleaning up after me; and of course my wife, Lucy, and daughter, Nikki, who served as my in-house information technology and support staff.

All of the historic images used are from the collection of the Peabody Historical Society and Museum, while the modern images are from the author's collection.

INTRODUCTION

It has been my stated purpose to use this book not only to reminisce about how things used to be but also to illustrate just how far those historic landscapes we appreciate have changed. I travel throughout the cities and towns of eastern Massachusetts on business and am continually struck by how many of our historic structures have changed over time, particularly in our cities. For example, many of the historic structures that were built for one or two families have been converted to apartments, causing the interior and exterior elements that gave the building its original character to be altered. That character was what once defined the neighborhood. It is often difficult to find a balance between historic preservation and modern business interests. The vintage and contemporary images in this book will show in sharp contrast how Peabody has changed throughout its long history.

CHAPTER 1

The Square, or the Center of It All

The view of the square from lower Main Street, as seen through the lens of Albion Low's camera in 1902, has really not changed all that much during the intervening 106 years. The Old South Congregational Church has moved to Prospect Street and been replaced by the Peabody District Courthouse. The Civil War monument memorializing those men from Peabody who died fighting in "the Great Rebellion" was moved closer to the new courthouse during a reconfiguration of traffic patterns in the square.

It is difficult to tell what time of year this 1890s photograph was taken. The smithies stand in their shirtsleeves, while their customers are wearing blankets. The men may have welcomed the cold as a respite from the intense heat generated by the forge inside. Then located on Railroad Avenue, Roger H. Smith went on to found an automotive supply store around the corner on Lowell Street.

This 50-foot-tall granite monument dedicated to the 71 soldiers and sailors from Peabody who were killed in action during the Civil War is topped by a statue of America modeled on a similar figure that sits atop the Capitol building in Washington, D.C. There is a tablet on the north side with the following inscription: "From The Town To her Sons Who Died In the Great Rebellion, That The Union Might Be Preserved and Liberty Secured To All."

Dashing through the square in a one-horse open sleigh—one can just hear the sleigh bells jingling as this couple makes its way across an almost-deserted Peabody Square around 1902. In this picture snapped by Mrs. J. Edward Osborn of 56 Washington Street, the spire of St. John's Catholic Church and the roof of Peabody's town hall are visible, while the Civil War monument, dedicated in 1881, dominates the square then as it does now. To its left can be seen a streetcar entering the square. The large building on the left was the home of the Standard Thermometer and Electric Company. Founded in 1885, the large factory produced innovative metallic thermometers, which were sold throughout the world. This space is now Liberty Park.

Like every village, city, and town in the late 1800s, Peabody had its share of train stations and crossing shacks. They have all disappeared, as have the trains they once served. There were, at one time, three different rail companies passing through either Peabody Square or West Peabody Junction on Pine Street. Eventually they were consolidated under the banner of the Boston and Maine Railroad (B&M). This early view is of Peabody's main station located on Central Street at the current site of the municipal parking lot and Dunkin' Donuts.

The Peabody Historical Society issued this early postcard view of the buildings comprising part of the St. John's Catholic Church complex on Church Street in 1905. The parish was founded in 1870, with the church, the largest in Peabody, completed in 1879. At the center is the parish's first schoolhouse, erected in 1893, and to the left of that is the convent of the Sisters of Notre Dame, built in 1895.

This photograph, taken on a beautiful morning around 1910, portrays a busy scene in the square. The trolley to Salem advertises, "Fun and Frolic at the Pit on Revere Beach" and two shows playing later that day at the Salem Willows Theatre. In the background, one can make out the marquee of the Olympic, Peabody's first movie theater. Built in 1908, the Olympic had six shows a day and was in business until around 1915 when competition from the much larger and more modern Strand Theater, which opened on Main Street in 1912, proved to be too much.

Taken from in front of the old Warren National Bank building, this mid-1920s look at the square during winter shows Manning's Lunch on the corner of Foster Street and the hose tower of the fire department's central station in the background. Across the street on the right, one can see Klemm's Bakery, Hamblett Hardware Company, and the Old South Congregational Church, with the Thomas block in the foreground on the right.

This early picture of the E. W. Upton block on the corner of Foster Street and Peabody Square, taken on June 14, 1919, shows the building all dressed up and ready to celebrate the end of World War I the previous November. The block housed many businesses over the years, such as Manning's Lunch at street level, the Standard Thermometer and Electric Company, Kirstien's Leather Company on the second and third floors, and Upton's Hall on the fourth floor. The Upton block survived until the 1960s.

This B&M passenger train crossed Peabody Square with stops at Newhall's Crossing, Vaughn's Station, Lynnfield Center, and Wakefield Junction and continued on to Boston. Originally the South Reading Line, the B&M took over this and most of the other smaller lines north of Boston by 1900.

CHAPTER 2

Ye Common Land Highway, or Main Street

Judging by the lack of foliage and the direction of the shadows cast by the trees in this view of Main Street facing the square, it must be a late morning in fall or winter. One is struck by the lack of any sign of people or vehicular traffic on the street. Perhaps it is Sunday, but one cannot help but be a little envious of the serene look this photograph depicts in comparison to what is now a very busy and often noisy thoroughfare.

It is difficult to tell where in the sequence of events surrounding the American funeral of George Peabody that this photograph fits. Is the body of Peabody arriving at the Peabody Institute Library to begin his period of lying in state? The horse-drawn trolleys seem to be waiting for passengers, who may have come from Salem to pay their respects. It is a snowy day in February 1870. The sleighs are lined up in front of the institute, which is appropriately festooned with funerary bunting.

Albert H. Whidden founded his hardware and tanning supply business located at 18 Main Street in 1874. It was adjacent to his family home at No. 20, just visible to the right. Whidden's brother Henry operated a butter and egg store at that location for many years. The hardware store was in business until 1964 when its longtime neighbor, the Warren Five Cents Savings Bank, bought the properties and expanded its operations. In this picture, dating from the 1890s, one can see that the second floor was home to the Women's Christian Temperance Union.

When A. H. Whidden Hardware moved next door to a larger facility in 1900, the New England Grocery Company opened its doors at 18 Main Street. J. H. Gates managed this particular branch. Before the emergence of the giant chain supermarkets, New England Grocery Company was for many years one of the largest grocery retail and wholesale businesses in the region. It was the corporate entity behind the Elm Farm Stores, one of the area's first successful supermarket chains. The store was gone from this location by 1910. This early picture shows the grocery company's fine delivery wagon and the staff posing on what appears to be, from the look of the bunting, a patriotic holiday.

The popular haberdashery operated at 25 Main Street by George H. Jacobs was the premier men's clothier in Peabody for a number of years. Founded in 1884, Jacobs's store boasted that it carried the finest gent's furnishing goods, along with hats, trunks, and bags in Peabody, as well as in its stores in Danvers and Livermore Falls, Maine. The store was eventually sold to Lucien Lewis and continued in business at this location until 1938 when it was destroyed by fire.

The church of the Second Universalist Society of Danvers was completed at the end of Walker Place in January 1832. Universalism was based on a belief in the inherent goodness and dignity of man. The society was first organized in America in 1793. Its liberal views for the time quickly spread across the country. The Universalists merged with the Unitarian Church in 1961. This church building, which backed up to Mill Street, was destroyed by fire. Walker Place was for many years set off 30 Main Street and is now the entrance to a parking lot.

The N. W. Edson grocery store located at 58 and 60 Main Street is seen in this picture from the 1890s. Edson's was one of the many local grocers in business downtown in the days before the arrival of large chain stores. These gentlemen appear to be employees, happy to step outside to have their picture taken. In the background is the Peabody Institute Library. Today the building long known as the Sutton block houses the Peabody Music Box among other businesses.

The Warren National Bank was founded in 1832 and named after the hero of the battle of Bunker Hill, Gen. Joseph Warren. The upper floors have been home to many organizations and businesses since then, particularly the Burdett Business School, the Peabody Historical Society, the Jordan lodge of Masons, and so many more. The bank eventually merged with Merchants Bank and then became part of the Shawmut Bank and on and on. The old bank is now the site of North of Boston Visitor's Center and the offices of Congressman John Tierney.

This large Second Empire–style house is situated on the corner of Park and Winter Streets. It was once the home of J. F. Clement, the owner of the Clement Machine Works located on the corner of Wallis and Walnut Streets, which later evolved into the Boyle Machine Company. The once fine home shares the fate that has befallen so many large, beautiful period homes in nearly every large city, namely, the sacrifice of the very structural elements that once gave the building its original identity and character.

The Ebenezer Sutton estate was situated directly across from the Peabody Institute Library on Main Street. Ebenezer (Eben) Sutton, along with his distinguished brother Gen. William Sutton was one of the wealthiest men in town. He was the owner of the Sutton Woolen Mills in Peabody and North Andover. Eben died in 1864. His two sons preceded him in death, and his large estate was passed to his wife, Eliza. The house eventually became the property of the Prevear family of Lynn. Interestingly the house may still be glimpsed behind the storefronts on the corner of Little's Lane and Main Street.

The Peabody Institute Library was built in South Danvers in 1854 and was named for its benefactor, George Peabody. Peabody, America's first great philanthropist, contributed a substantial part of his sizable fortune to more than 30 educational and humanitarian institutions that still bear his name throughout the world. The Italian villa–style institute was the most popular subject of early photographers in town, and it has served as the cultural focal point of the city since it was built. This particularly striking view was taken in August 1896.

President of the Peabody Camera Club, George Low took this photograph of the whitewashed brick building located at 108 Main Street around 1900. At that time, it was occupied by Horace A. Bushby and Sons Grocery. Built in 1830, it is one of the earliest buildings remaining in Peabody's downtown. Prior to the Bushby store, it housed the then popular fraternal organization known as the Odd Fellows. In later years, a restaurant run by Demetrios Petranos was on the ground floor, with apartments above. The contemporary picture shows that the historic structure now houses a cell phone store. The building continues to exhibit its original Federal characteristics. The house to the right is the B. F. Wheeler house, which has been lovingly maintained in nearly original condition by the people at the North Shore Community Action Programs (NSCAP).

The first bank to be established in town was the South Danvers National Bank in 1825. The older photograph, taken in 1890, shows the second home of the bank at the corner of Holten and Main Streets. By 1892, the bank moved into its new headquarters at 22 Main Street. Just eight years later, the bank was closed due to mismanagement. The losses totaled approximately $230,000. Most of the depositors, both businesses and individuals, lost all their money. After an investigation, the head cashier, George Foster, and his assistant, John Dickinson, were indicted in federal court in 1902. In 1913, due to a calamitous series of events, the charges were dropped. The brick Federal-style building at 125 Main Street is now the site of Dr. Robert Stein's dental office.

The Peabody Community House was located on the old Shaw estate at 10 Holten Street from 1915 to 1924. It was established in an attempt by the city to provide a safe, structured environment for the children of Peabody to play sports and participate in classes related to woodworking, cooking, folk dancing, target shooting, and so on. It was reported that in 1917, youths made over 20,000 combined visits to the facility. Even though it seemed to be a success, it was shut down in 1924 due to a lack of committed leadership.

Elizabeth Whitman, the real-life subject of *The Coquette*, one of America's first successful novels by a woman, is buried here under a stone whose poignant epitaph so eloquently tells her tale. Whitman, whose name was changed to Eliza Wharton in the novel, came to the Bell Tavern on Main Street for a room to await the birth of her child. While waiting for her baby's father to arrive, she spent her time writing heartrending poetry and prose. She waited to no avail and died soon after she gave birth to her stillborn child. Her friends and family erected a gravestone that was chipped away by fans of the book as souvenirs, eventually wearing it away to a mere nub. The Peabody Historical Commission and the Peabody Institute Library erected a facsimile stone in 2005.

The cemetery on the other side of these old iron gates has been known by many names since its inception in 1663. It has been called the Old Main Street Burying Ground, Trask's Burial Ground, and the Old South Cemetery. Among the hundreds buried there are 17 veterans of the Revolutionary War, 4 of whom were killed at Menotomy during the battle of Lexington and Concord. Also interred here is Capt. Dennison Wallis, who survived being wounded numerous times in the same skirmish and returned home to begin a long, prosperous career in the leather business.

CHAPTER 3

Gape's Lane and Ye County Road, or Central and Andover Streets

Peabody Square was the epicenter of most activities in town prior to the evolution of Route 114 and the opening of the Northshore Mall in 1958. Here is a crowd milling about, making its way to the Emerson Park area to visit the Essex Agricultural Fair. The fair was held in Peabody for many years prior to moving to Topsfield.

As one may see from the early photograph, the junction of Walnut and Central Streets has always been a busy commercial corner in downtown. In 1904, A. P. Ames operated a retail feed and grain store, taking over the Day and Richardson Company, which had previously succeeded the J. V. Hanson Company established in 1851. The still attractive Rosenfeldt building was erected on this site in 1916 and housed many businesses and tenants over the years. The fraternal organization the Loyal Order of Moose No. 1450 had its meeting hall upstairs for many years and Skal's, a popular bar and restaurant, was located here as well. The Fire Bull Restaurant, featuring Brazilian barbecue, is now situated on the corner.

This original building was constructed on Stevens Street in 1856 and served as both the first town hall and the high school for the newly created South Danvers. This classic Greek Revival–style building replaced the first George Peabody High School that had been founded in 1850 and was housed in a small building in Park Square. Prior to that year, there was no high school, as all students were taught in one of the one-room schoolhouses scattered throughout the town. Municipal offices were moved to the new Peabody City Hall in 1883, and the high school expanded. When more room was needed, a new high school was built on Central Street in 1903. The upper story was razed after a fire. It has served as the headquarters of the Fidelity Post 1011 Peabody Veterans of Foreign Wars since 1924.

Mrs. Samuel L. Cassino took this picture of the Victorian-era home located at 10 Stevens Street from her own yard across the street. The house has retained most of its original ornamental detail, such as the cornices above the windows and the attractive and functional sentry box-style front doorway. Note the beautiful design of the fence in front with its lattice gate. To the right, the original high school and town hall can be seen through the trees. The owner of the house at that time was Jacob Osborn. He owned many fine properties in town, including over 60 acres of scattered woodlands. In the 1800s, Osborn family members owned just about every house in the Central Street area.

This early view of the corner of Elm and Central Streets shows the home of America's first candy company, the George W. Pepper Company. Established in 1830, it was famous for a type of candy known as Gibraltar's, which is still made today. When George W. Pepper bought the business in 1864, he moved it to 4 Elm Street. There it prospered and shipped its product throughout the world. The company still exists on Derby Street in Salem. The boy on the right of the picture is pulling what may well be a Goodwill Soap cart. The Marsh family manufactured this soap on Summit Street in Peabody for many years, as well as in Lynn. It was sold door-to-door by boys from their carts and provided these young entrepreneurs a means to supplement their families' incomes. The house on the right now houses the Courthouse Pub. In the distance the gates of the Monumental Cemetery on Wallis Street can be seen.

The Reverend Benjamin Prescott was seemingly a complicated man who was born in Concord in 1689, graduated from Harvard College in 1709, and was appointed the first minister of the Old South Congregational Church in 1713. From that time on, he had an often contentious relationship with his congregation, usually concerning money. Starting at £80 per year, he asked for and received increases up to £620 per year over time. The Prescott house was built in 1750 as a wedding gift to Prescott and his third wife, Mary, by her brother Sir William Pepperell, the provisional governor of the colony. The house, with all its impressive accoutrements, was greatly damaged by fire and eventually torn down shortly thereafter. It is now the site of the Prescott Apartments at 72 Central Street.

When the second George Peabody High School on Stevens Street proved inadequate, an initiative was undertaken to build a new high school in 1899. The school, complete with 25 classrooms and an auditorium, was opened on September 1, 1904. It was thought at the time that this facility would serve the needs of Peabody's students for at least 50 years; however, an addition was needed by 1920. Eventually the handsome buff brick building served as the Seeglitz Junior High when a new high school was built on Allen's Lane in 1966. That building quickly became the Higgins Middle School when the present-day Veteran's Memorial High School was opened in 1971.

Peabody was one of the earliest centers of pottery manufacturing in America. At one time, the names of Osborn, Southwick, Goldthwaite, and Wilson were prominent among those who made their living as potters. The town's close proximity to the beds along the Water's River helped to insure a steady supply of clay. An old road to these beds can still be seen behind 175 Andover Street as it passes the gate of the Wilson Cemetery. The local pottery business declined after 1820 when people began to move west, taking the trade with them. Moses B. Paige learned his trade at Reed Pottery. Paige bought out Jacob Reed in 1876 and owned the business until the 1950s when a spectacular fire destroyed the building. The site is now the home of the Aheppa House, a senior housing facility built by the Daughters of Penelope.

This early picture of the Nathaniel Bowditch School, once located at 84 Central Street, shows what may be the most attractive elementary school ever built in the city. Built in 1858 to replace an earlier district schoolhouse, this classic Italianate-style structure with its characteristic cube shape, cupola, and arched windows is further enhanced by the dual pilasters decoratively supporting the roof. The gentleman in the foreground seems to be reading a periodical while, perhaps, waiting for a streetcar. The school was later the home of the American Legion post until it was destroyed by fire.

A Mr. Goldwaithe is credited with taking this photograph of Wilson Square for inclusion in the Peabody Historical Society's Century Chest time capsule, created in 1902. The Benjamin Wilson house is in the center, with his son Clark Wilson's home, which still exists today, to its left. Benjamin, his wife, a daughter, and a son are buried in a small cemetery on Pulaski Street that was recently reclaimed by the Peabody Historical Commission.

This 1902 image of the aforementioned Clark Wilson house at 5 Andover Street is graced by the presence of the two little girls sitting atop the fence corner posts. The Second Empire–style dwelling soon became the home of Daniel B. Lord, a prosperous plumber and steamfitter who opened a plumbing supply shop at 19 Foster Street. The house was long ago turned into commercial real estate and, though well maintained, has lost much of its original character. In recent years, it was home to Alice Vega Gowns. It is now the site of a computer sales business.

This early photograph, dating from the 1890s, shows a group of boys playing under the elm trees in Wilson Square on what was then known as Pine Tree Corner. One boy leans on a water trough. The sign reads, "Lynn 6 m" and "Boston 14 m" In the background is the Nathaniel Bowditch Jr. house, which was built about 1761. While the house was owned by many generations of the Osborn family, its most noteworthy inhabitant was Bowditch. Bowditch lived here with his family for about five years. He went on to write a book on celestial navigation, titled *The Practical Navigator*, which is still in use today.

This early photograph shows the corner of Andover, Liberty (Pulaski), Endicott, and Central Streets, which has long been known as Wilson Square in honor of the many families of that name who lived in the area. These boys are sitting on a water trough next to a rock being used a billboard to advertise Gillilands Liniment, which was at one time made nearby in Danvers.

The Elias Hasket Derby summer estate was located at the corner of present-day Buttonwood Lane and Andover Street. Originally called Apple Tree Lane, the road continued on to the estate of his daughter Elizabeth Derby West and her husband, Capt. Nathaniel West, which was located at the present site of the Northshore Mall. Legendary master builder Samuel McIntire of Salem designed the main house and barns. The barns were disassembled and moved to Watertown in the 1920s, while the main house was torn down in the 1970s. This early view of the entrance to the lane and farm was taken on September 22, 1895.

Oak Hill was the name given to the estate on Andover Street owned by the Wests. It was built on land inherited by Elizabeth from Derby, her father, who was considered the wealthiest man in the country before his death in 1799. It was arguably the largest and most finely appointed home in the area, with woodwork and mantels designed by McIntire and magnificent murals. The Wests soon divorced, and upon Elizabeth's death, two large sections of the house were disassembled and moved to Salem where they were incorporated into Nathaniel's mansion on Chestnut Street.

The magnificent Oak Hill became the property of the Rogers family in 1850. The family spent large sums of money on returning the main house to its former splendor. The grounds, totaling about 200 acres, were exquisitely designed to resemble English gardens, complete with lily ponds and tree-lined drives that circled back to Andover Street. Jacob Rogers, who was a partner in the firm of J. P. Morgan, the successor of George Peabody's firm, lived in the house until his death. When his widow, Elizabeth Peabody Rogers, died in 1921, the property was sold to the Xaverian Brothers religious order. The Xaverian Brothers sold it to Allied Stores in 1955. The house was torn down and the Northshore Shopping Center, now called the Northshore Mall, opened on the site in 1958.

CHAPTER 4

MOUNT PLEASANT AND FELTON'S CORNER, OR BROOKSBY FARM

This massive shingle-style house was the summer residence of David M. Little and his family, who were from Salem. The house may have been designed by Little's brother, Arthur, of the noted Boston firm Little and Brown. David Little served as mayor of Salem in 1900. He was also a naval architect, a lieutenant commander in World War I, and a photographer. The home was razed sometime in the middle of the 20th century, most likely to make way for the construction of Route 128.

The first organized school system in the town of Danvers began with the institution of the district or neighborhood schools in the 1800s. District School No. 6 was built in 1841 on Sylvan Street and, with the abolition of the district system, it was renamed the Felton School. It served as such until the 1930s. It still stands and has been used for a myriad of commercial ventures, including a bank and, most recently, a flower store.

In the latter part of the 19th century, Joseph Newhall Smith, who grew up on a farm in the Goodale Street area, made a fortune manufacturing shoes in nearby Lynn. He invested his money in energy and mining stocks and became a very wealthy man. He bought Brooksby Farm from the Felton family, and he, his children, and his grandchildren used the farm as their summer home for many years. This photograph from about 1916 is of his granddaughter Janet Smith, who, upon her death in 1983, graciously willed this part of the property to the Peabody Historical Society and Museum.

The Nathaniel Felton Sr. house was begun in 1644 and evolved into the house shown in this photograph from 1900. Felton made his way up the North River from Salem to Peabody Square in the late 1630s to claim a land grant given to his mother, Ellen. After years spent clearing the land atop Mount Pleasant, he began to build his house and create a prosperous life for his family and his descendants. The Feltons lived in the house until 1910 when it became the property of the Smith family. It is now the property of the Peabody Historical Society and Museum.

The intersection of Sylvan, Prospect, and Andover Streets was once known as Felton's Corner. This particular Felton house was home to Nathan Felton, who, through the years, served as state representative, town clerk, town selectman, school committee member, and collector of taxes. Nathan also found time to run a general store located on the opposite corner. The Felton Cemetery can be seen farther up the hill under the trees. This cemetery supplanted an earlier family burial ground dating back to the 1650s and is the final resting place for generations of Feltons, with the earliest known burial in 1792.

This is the same intersection as in the previous picture but looking down Prospect Street across Andover Street (Route 114) toward Sylvan Street. The roads have been widened considerably, and the houses have been replaced with commercial buildings. The Just for Pets store replaced the Daniel Felton farm on this corner.

Thorndike Proctor built this Federal-style house, located at 54 Prospect Street, around 1818. It was constructed on the former site of the James Houlton house, which had been destroyed by fire. It was in the Houlton house in 1709 that the first organized classes for the children of Peabody were held. The first teacher was Katherine Daland. In 1910, a plaque acknowledging Daland's contribution to the establishment of the Peabody school system was erected in front of the house. The granite post to which it is attached is visible in both pictures on the home's front lawn.

At one time, Mount Pleasant, or what is now called the Brooksby Farm area of town between Andover, Lowell, and Prospect Streets, was covered in northern fruit trees. The earlier photograph is of the Emmerton Cider Mill where some of that fruit was processed into cider. The mill was torn down and the present house was built on the foundation. According to historian Dan Doucette, the basement of the house still contains some of the machinery used in cider making so many years ago.

Jordan Marsh department stores were founded in Boston in 1841. They grew into a retailing powerhouse in the New England area and eventually merged with Macy's, a sister division within Allied Stores. Allied was the originator of the Northshore Shopping Center, which was built on the site of the Derby-Rogers estate in 1958 as the first regional mall in New England. For 50 years, Jordan Marsh, along with Filene's, served as a premier destination store at the mall.

James W. Wilkins, together with his brother Fred, ran this successful farm, dairy, and butchery at 349 Lowell Street near Proctor's Crossing for many years. His sister Helen Wilkins was a teacher at the Rockville School in South Peabody, while his sister Julia taught at the Center School on Franklin Street.

CHAPTER 5

Olde Boston Road, or Washington Street

Steven Blaney was one of the most successful men in town in the latter part of the 1800s. He was a partner in the leather and wool business of Winchester and Blaney on Walnut Street and served as president of the Warren Five Cents Savings Bank. This large estate at 196 Washington Street was most beautifully landscaped with gardens that were the envy of everyone in town. The house is still there, but the rest of the estate has been broken up for house lots.

Hundreds of people gathered at the intersection of Washington and Main Streets on April 19, 1902, to commemorate the anniversary of the battle of Lexington and Concord and honor those men from Peabody who lost their lives that day at Menotomy (Arlington Heights). In 1894, April 19 was officially recognized in Massachusetts as Patriot's Day, and since that time, the Peabody Historical Society has continued to honor these men and their holiday with an appropriate celebration. The monument was moved to a new location on the corner of Washington and Sewell Streets in the early 1970s after it proved to be a traffic hazard.

Josiah B. Thomas, a Peabody meatpacking and leather-manufacturing magnate, built this outstanding example of the Colonial Revival style of architecture as a wedding present for his grandson Elmer Thomas in 1898. Located at 2 Washington Street, the house is today part of the city's Washington Street Historic District. Josiah died shortly before the house was finished. He was born in Halifax in 1827. He came to Peabody in 1861 and began to develop a financial empire that was unrivaled in the city. In addition to meats, his integrated manufacturing interests included the tanning of sheepskins, wool, shoes, and boxes.

The Lexington monument was erected in 1835 to memorialize the seven men from Danvers who were killed at Arlington Heights on April 19, 1775, by the British who were marching back to Boston from action at Concord. The names of George Southwick, Benjamin Deland, Samuel Cook, Ebenezer Goldthwait, and Henry Jacobs from South Danvers, as well as Jotham Webb and Perley Putnam from the north section of town, are etched into the granite obelisk hewed at the nearby Brown's Quarry.

Dole and Osgood was one of four carriage and wagon manufacturers located in Peabody in the late 1800s. Established by Moses Dole as a blacksmith shop in 1822, the carriage business blossomed under the aegis of his son William T. Dole, who joined the company in 1834. William eventually formed a partnership with W. E. Osgood and together manufactured and sold their products around the world. They apparently had a contract with the then popular Moxie tonic company, whose advertising prominently adorns the wagons in the early scene. The building with a new facade, located at 13 Washington Street, became the home of the Pioneer Garage.

The Federal-style Gen. Gideon Foster House was built around 1815, is located at 35 Washington Street, and has been the headquarters of the Peabody Historical Society and Museum since 1916. Foster, a patriot, led a company of militia in the battle of Lexington and Concord, the siege of Boston, and the battle of Bunker Hill. After the war, he designed and built chocolate, grist, and bark mills on Goldthwaite's Brook on the street that bears his name. Foster held many prominent positions in the town during his remarkable life of 96 years. He died in 1845 and is buried in Harmony Grove Cemetery under a monument paid for in part by George Peabody.

A proud Mr. and Mrs. J. Edward Osborn seem eager to take a ride in their new, presumably rare, automobile in this 1902 picture taken for inclusion in the Peabody Historical Society's Century Chest. The Osborns lived in fine style at 56 Washington Street and were principals in the leather-manufacturing firm of J. E. and J. H. Osborn located at 37 Foster Street. The company's main office at that time was situated at 128 Summer Street in Boston. The barn is gone now, and the once grand single-family home has been converted into six apartments.

In this 1890s-era photograph, boys are casually perched atop the fence waiting patiently as their picture is recorded. The Second Empire–style house that is pictured was built around 1870 on the corner of Washington Street and Washington Place for the Willey family. Since then, most of the ornamentation has been discarded, though the pedimented cornice window heads are still evident above the dormers, but the cornices above the lower windows are gone. The ornamental double brackets along the eaves have disappeared as well. The slate mansard roof has been replaced with asphalt shingles, and the house's clapboards have been replaced with aluminum siding.

This picture, taken in the 1890s, shows a sleigh parked by the 18th-century farmhouse that was the birthplace of the city's namesake, George Peabody. Celebrated throughout the world as much for his humanitarian and philanthropic efforts as for his ability to generate a great deal of wealth, Peabody's generous donations were focused primarily in the areas of education and public welfare. The example he set served to bring others of his time, such as Johns Hopkins and Andrew Carnegie, to the realization that with wealth and privilege comes the responsibility to help those less fortunate than themselves. The home is now the site of the recently renovated George Peabody House Museum. Visit the museum to find out more information about the life and works of this fascinating man.

This pastoral view was titled "90 degrees in the shade" by its photographer, Annie Newhall. Newhall lived with her mom nearby at 117 Lynnfield Street. It is noted on the back of the photograph that the cows belonged to William Reed, who resided at 50 Lynn Street. The bull is warily eyeing Newhall as she gets her shot. In the background is the railroad track of the old South Reading Railroad, which maintained service from Peabody Square past Newhall's Crossing through Lynnfield Center to Wakefield Junction (South Reading).

Written on the back of this photograph from around 1900 is the title "Great Elm at the junction of Lynn and Lynnfield Streets." The large house and barn in the foreground was the home of Charles H. Putnam at 1 Lynn Street. To the right is another Putnam house on Lynnfield Street. Note the telephone and electric poles bringing electricity to what was primarily farmland. This pastoral scene is in striking contrast to the busy intersection one sees today.

The difference between the look of the Summit Street of old and that of today is amazing. The early photographer was standing near the entrance to what is now Capone's restaurant, facing west. Summit Street was originally part of what was known as Olde Ipswich Road, which ran from South Peabody down Summit Street to Prospect Street on to Sylvan Street, eventually terminating in Ipswich.

CHAPTER 6

SOUTHWICK'S LANE, OR LOWELL STREET

Ebenezer and Betsey Upton King built this house, located at 193 Lowell Street, in 1810. It is one of many large homes built by the storied King family along Lowell Street in the 17th and 18th centuries. It passed into the hands of James A. King by 1890. James was one of the most prosperous men in the county and owned over 250 acres of land in Peabody alone. He served for a time as the head of the Peabody Electric Light plant. Perhaps it is James and his family, replete with dog and horses, seen posing in this early photograph taken from across the street. The barn was taken down in 1929. The house remains in the King family and is currently owned by society member Jeff Mercer.

The stately Peabody City Hall was built in 1883 in the Second Empire style that was so prevalent in municipal buildings constructed in the last third of the 19th century. It is nearly original and has recently undergone a sensitive renovation by the Bonfanti Administration that has revitalized and enhanced the building's connections to the city's celebrated past.

The school day had just begun on the morning of October 28, 1915, when a disastrous fire broke out at St. John's Parochial School and ended with the tragic loss of 21 students. A local photographer captured the horrific fire, as the gathered crowd stood helplessly by. In 2005, a beautiful memorial honoring those victims of the fire was dedicated through the efforts of the St. John's parish family and the Peabody Historical Society.

This busy scene from the 1920s is of the Roger H. Smith Auto Supply store located next to the Peabody Fire Department's central station at 35 Lowell Street. The Smiths started out as blacksmiths and successfully made the transition from horses to the horseless carriage. They lived for many years at 205 Lowell Street. As one can see, they sold Hood, Goodyear, and Firestone tires, Eveready batteries, and Mobil products. Note the early gas pump in the foreground and the solid rubber tires standing in front of the store. Their service car in the background is equipped with these hard-riding, albeit durable, tires.

The Sawyer house, then located at 83 Lowell Street and facing Peabody Square, was home to the Peabody branch of one of the earliest families to settle in Salem. The Sawyers were in the meat-processing business. The slaughterhouse and packing plant was located on their property near the current central fire station. Many generations of the Sawyer family lived on the farm, some of which may be seen posing on the front lawn in this picture from the early 20th century. It appears as though the barn has survived as the small house on the right of the recent picture. The property is now the site of the Red Cross building and parking lot at 85 Lowell Street.

At his death in 1898, Josiah B. Thomas left $50,000 to the town of Peabody to create a community hospital. Ultimately that hospital was built on King Street with the first patient being admitted on October 25, 1907. The individual patient rooms were furnished by both individuals and community-based organizations. The Thomas estate made an additional contribution of $40,000 in 1914. In later years, the hospital incurred ever-increasing losses until it was decided by the Torigian administration that the city could no longer afford to remain in control of the institution. A buyer was found, and the hospital became an acute-care facility. The Lahey Clinic North now serves the city.

The John Southwick house at 151 Lowell Street was built in 1660 by the son of Lawrence and Casandra Southwick, both of whom were victims of the Quaker persecution of the 1650s. The local sheriff attempted to sell John's sister Provided Southwick into slavery in a failed attempt to satisfy the fines placed upon her family for their religious infidelity. Provided's tragic story, albeit misnamed, is the basis of Quaker poet John Greenleaf Whittier's poem *Cassandra Southwick*. This early episode of intolerance was a precursor to the witchcraft delusion a mere 40 years later.

The Edmund Batters house, parts of which most likely date from the mid-1600s, is located at 220 Lowell Street and is one of the earliest homes in Peabody. Batters, who lived near Townhouse Square in Salem, was granted 112 acres of land in 1637. The property eventually became part of the King family estate until purchased by Enoch Page in 1827. The parcel at that time included Clark's Hill on Summit Street, which quickly became known as Page's Hill. Page's Hill was for many years the site of a popular local ski area. The house went through a series of prominent owners during the late 19th and the 20th centuries.

Samuel King built this beautiful home, located on the west corner of Forest and Lowell Streets, in 1846. It is on the former site of a house and store owned by his parents, Zachariah and Desire Jacobs King. The King family first arrived in Peabody in 1636 and quickly rose to prominence as grocers and distributors of vinegar, rum, and frozen hogs. The family used the fortune they acquired from this business to buy up huge tracts of land in Essex County and became, for a time, the largest landowners in the area. The Kings played a prominent role in Peabody life for over 300 years. The extended family built and owned many of the large houses located along present-day Lowell Street.

The Peabody Historical Society erected the Proctor memorial at the junction of Summit and Lowell Streets in 1902 on the same day the vintage photograph was taken. The memorial commemorates the death of John Proctor, "a Martyr to the Truth," who was tried and convicted of being a wizard during the Salem witchcraft hysteria. Proctor was hanged on August 19, 1692. His wife, Elizabeth, was spared the same fate by virtue of her being pregnant at the time of their trial. She delivered their baby two weeks after his death.

Emmanuel Downing first built a house on this site at 348 Lowell Street as early as 1638. The present Proctor house was begun in 1650. Downing operated a tavern here until he leased the 300-acre farm to his neighbor John Proctor in 1666. Proctor continued to run the inn until both he and his wife, Elizabeth, were arrested for allegedly consorting with the devil. The current owners of the home have recently begun a historically sensitive restoration.

In 1900, when 11-year-old Francis Whitten Jr. of Malden took this picture of the old Salem and Lowell Railroad's Proctor station, one could catch the train here at the corner of Prospect and Lowell Streets beneath the present-day Temple Ner Tamid to the West Peabody station on Pine Street. There one could change trains for Boston and the rest of the country or continue on to Lowell via the old rail bed that runs along Russell Street through Middleton, North Reading, Wilmington, and Tewksbury.

CHAPTER 7

West Danvers, or West Peabody

The Annie Geary home, located in the woods on the west side of Lake Street, was the scene of Geary's vicious murder in 1898. Although the case was never solved, there was rampant speculation that the culprit was the ne'er-do-well son of a local minister. Shortly after, he went to the state penitentiary for a series of crimes committed in the West Peabody area.

The intersection of Lowell and Newbury Streets was once markedly different than that which exists today. Newbury Street (Route 1) meandered about 100 yards west of where it is today, to the left of the house with the two bay windows seen in both photographs. The old road once continued north behind the mobile home parks and Circuit City into modern-day Danvers, and it is now the entrance to the present-day North East Nursery.

When Sarah P. Flint married future congressman Daniel P. King in 1824, they moved into this beautiful home on her family's estate. Originally built during the American Revolution, this Colonial gambrel house still commands a view of Crystal Lake from the corner of Lowell and Goodale Streets. King served as a state senator, state representative, and speaker of the Massachusetts house. An ardent abolitionist, he was elected to the U.S. Congress in 1843. The home changed hands over the years and was most recently the location of Miss Fay's Country Day School, once operated by the Morris Ankeles family. Although the property is to be developed, the old farmhouse will be preserved.

This postcard, printed by the Peabody Historical Society in 1902, shows the West School and the West Congregational Church that were located at the corner of West and Taylor Streets in West Peabody. West Street was renamed in honor of Eben Johnson, who was killed during World War I. The church was organized in 1883 as a branch of the Rockville Congregational Church in South Peabody. The Italianate-style schoolhouse was constructed in 1870 to replace two old district schools. The school contained two classrooms on the first floor with a hall above. Schoolhouse Hall, as it was known, served as the meeting place for a number of West Peabody groups and events.

The West Peabody train station was located on an extension off Pine Street. Over the years, the station served as the site of the West Peabody Post Office and an American Express office. American Express started in 1850 and originally forwarded freight by rail. From that business evolved the financial powerhouse it is today. The little village included the West Peabody firehouse and Daniel Brown's grocery store. Note the vintage automobile and its passenger awaiting the train or perhaps doing business with the post office.

The early village of Brookdale was centered at the confluence of Winona, Pine, and Lake Streets in West Peabody. This corner, now known locally as Five Corners, had its own train station, post office, and firehouse on Pine Street. Brookdale Hall, which was located above Joseph Brown's store on Winona Street, served as the community center for the village. Brookdale was also the location of the Winona Woolen Mills and the Ingraham Morocco leather factory, both on the shores of Devil's Dishful Pond. At its height in 1889, the Ingraham factory was turning out more than 4,000 quality hides per week.

There were at least four mills built in the West Peabody area around Crystal Lake and Devil's Dishful Pond in the 17th and 18th centuries, taking advantage of the abundant streams and ponds in the area. There was the aforementioned woolen mill, as well as gristmills and sawmills. There has been a mill at the corner of Lake and Lowell Streets in West Peabody since 1681. The ruins can still be seen in the woods and are reputedly haunted by the ghosts of witchcraft persecution victims Giles and Martha Corey. If so, the Coreys may be a bit confused, as their mill was sited a short distance away near the intersection of Pine and Winona Streets.

As one can plainly see by the street sign, the subject of this vintage photograph, Crystal Lake Farm, was located at the corner of Lowell and Goodale Streets. The main house was built around 1875 on the spot of the mid-17th-century home of early settler Thomas Flint. The land was owned by the Carten family for many years and was primarily a dairy and livestock farm producing and distributing bottled milk, butter, and eggs. It sold dairy cows as well. The John Carten home became a nursing home in the late 1950s and was later destroyed by fire.

On a summer's day in 1902, it appears that Addie Brown has convinced her father, Daniel, to take out the skiff on Devil's Dishful Pond and pose for a picture to be included in the Peabody Historical Society's Century Chest. Daniel operated a grocery store and post office just up the road near the train station. He was once also the owner of Rockdale Park in South Peabody, the scene of many exciting horse races. The park, then located in the area of the street of the same name and St. Adelaide's, was sold to a developer in the 1940s.